Outdoor
Paint Effects

Outdoor
Paint
Effects

Susan Cohen

CREATIVE
PUBLISHING
international

MINNETONKA, MINNESOTA

First published in the USA and Canada by
Creative Publishing international, Inc.

5900 Green Oak Drive
Minnetonka, MN 55343
1-800-328-3895
www.howtobookstore.com

First published in United Kindom by
New Holland Publishers (UK) Ltd
London • Cape Town • Sydney • Auckland

Copyright © 2000 in text and designs Susan Cohen
Copyright © 2000 in photography New Holland Publishers (UK) Ltd
Copyright © 2000 New Holland Publishers (UK) Ltd

All rights reserved. No part of this publication may be reproduced,
stored in a retrieval system, or transmitted in any form or by any
means, electronic, mechanical, photocopying, recording or
otherwise, without the prior written permission of the publishers
and copyright holders.

ISBN 0-86573-166-7

Reproduction by Modern Age Repro House, Hong Kong
Printed and bound in Malaysia by Times Offset (M) Sdn Bhd

10 9 8 7 6 5 4 3 2 1

Important
The author and publishers have made every effort to ensure that all
instructions given in this book are safe and accurate. They cannot
accept liability for any resulting injury or loss or damage to either
property or person, whether direct or consequential and howsoever
arising. Nor can they accept responsibility for finished projects.
Materials, tools and skills vary greatly and are the responsibility of
the reader. Always read the manufacturer's instructions and carry
out the appropriate safety precautions.

CONTENTS

INTRODUCTION

Working on this book has been such fun for me, and, in a way, a great relief for my family. Ever since I started paint-finishing professionally some 11 years ago, they have resigned themselves to the fact that nothing – except Monty, our pet golden retriever – is sacred, and if anything in the house can be ragged, dragged, stippled or stencilled, it probably will be. With the garden as my new "canvas" they breathed a sigh of relief. At last they were out of the direct firing line, and readily accepted their new roles as pot movers and construction consultants.

The idea for the book came about when I was looking for ways of working outside of the traditional boundaries of paint-finishing. What better way to do this than by viewing the garden as an extension of the indoor living space – without the restrictions of furniture and furnishings, walls and windows. Start looking at and thinking about your garden in the same way and you will quickly realize, as I did, that there is tremendous creative potential in outdoor paint effects.

There are as many ways of adding atmosphere and style, color and texture to outside areas as there are to inside spaces, and there are very few surfaces that cannot be enhanced. Whether you have a garden, a yard, a terrace or a patio, you will soon see that its fixtures and fittings, as well as moveable items, can be decorated in a way that will enable you to

reinvent your garden. All you need is a little imagination.

From liming an oak tabletop to marbling a plaster column, from gilding a window trough to aging a plastic wall feature, the projects in this book encompass all manner of decorative paint techniques. Throughout the book you will find all the information you need to produce wonderful outdoor paint finishes. Starting with a look at suitable surfaces, there are details of the tools and materials you are likely to need, as well as advice on suitable paints, glazes and varnishes. You will also be introduced to some exciting, innovative commercial products that let you achieve unusual finishes. To make the projects as accessible as possible, each one includes easy-to-follow, step-by-step instructions, as well as a comprehensive list of the equipment required, a summary of the finish being created and information on preparing your surface. Some also offer alternative color combinations or variations for you to try.

GETTING STARTED

Starting out with the correct equipment and materials for a particular project is the first important step to success. Many of the projects in this book decorate the kind of items you will already have in the garden, others might encourage a visit to the garden center. The paints, brushes, glazes, and even some of the more unusual equipment like stamps, crackle glaze and patinating kits, can be found in many DIY stores. In a few cases, a trip to an art supply store will be necessary to find the more specialized materials like artists' oil and acrylic colors, fine artists' brushes and whiting powder.

The following pages will help you get to grips with the surfaces, preparation materials, brushes, paints, varnishes and specialized products you will encounter in the project section of the book.

When shopping for equipment, you will find that prices vary, especially where brushes are concerned. It is not always necessary to buy the most expensive, but any brush will last longer if you take care of it by cleaning it as soon as you have finished using it. Use water and detergent to wash off water-based products or mineral spirits for oil-based materials.

Suitable Surfaces for Outdoor Paint Effects

Chipped-paint effect

Traditionally associated with garden fencing, wood takes on a whole new identity when it is painted. Take stock of all the wooden objects in your garden and you will realize the potential at your fingertips. You can revive an old garden bench or bring glamour to the garden shed, and don't forget the gardener's favorite "hold-all", the humble garden trug.

Suggested items: *trellis, trellis arbors, benches, fencing, gates, bird houses, tabletops, garden shed, potting bench, log planters, decking, summerhouse, playhouse, picnic seats, deck-chair frames, garden trugs.*

Suitable finishes: *chipped-paint effect, crackle glaze, craquelure (works best on small items), freehand painting, liming (only suitable for raw or stripped hardwood with a natural grain, oak for example), marbling, oil glazing, patinating, stamping, two-tone dry-brushing, waxing, wax resist, wood staining, color wash.*

FERROUS (IRON) METAL

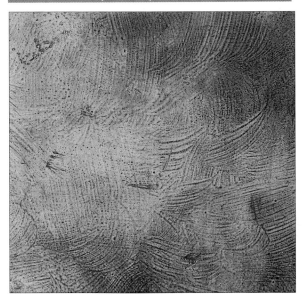

Patinated metal powders

There is a long-standing link between iron and the outdoors – a favorite material in the manufacture of gates and railings, it is also widely used for garden furniture. In an outdoor setting, aged metal has an impressive look that creates an aura of atmosphere and style. But why wait years for the elements to work their magic when you can recreate the look using decorative paint techniques?

Suggested items: *garden tables, benches and chairs, railings, gates, iron pots, metal wall brackets, candleholders.*

Suitable finishes: *bagging, craquelure (works best on small items), freehand painting (on painted metal), gilding (with metal leaf or metallic powders), marbling, oil glazing, patinating, rust effect, sparkle varnishing, stamping (on painted metal), verdigris effect, weathered-lead effect.*

NON-FERROUS METAL

Metal leaf

Galvanized metal, steel and tin containers come in all shapes and sizes, and make excellent garden planters. Inexpensive to buy, in its natural state the metal blends in with its surroundings, but can be decorated to make either a bold feature or a discreet statement.

Suggested items: *plant troughs, buckets, watering cans, florists' vases, milk pails, plant pots, reclaimed bath tubs.*

Suitable finishes: *bagging, craquelure (works best on small items), freehand painting (on painted metal), gilding (with metal leaf or metallic powders), marbling, oil glazing, patinating, rust effect, sparkle varnishing, stamping (on painted metal), verdigris effect, weathered-lead effect.*

TERRA COTTA

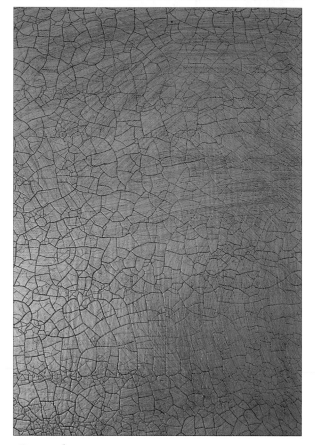

Craquelure

Hand-thrown or manufactured terra-cotta pots are the darling of gardeners all over the world. They can become focal points in the overall scheme, or provide a foil for the plants they contain. And don't overlook the use of decorated terra-cotta pots as candleholders. Remember, if you live in a cold climate you must buy frost-proof terra cotta which will not crack in extreme temperatures.

Suggested items: *plant pots of all shapes and sizes, statues, decorative items.*

Suitable finishes: *bagging, craquelure (works best on small items), freehand painting, gilding (with metal leaf), marbling, patinating, sandstone effect, sparkle varnishing, weathered-lead effect, weathered-terra-cotta effect.*

Weathered-terra-cotta effect

Verdigris effect

So you don't have garden steps set with hand-painted tiles, or a patio made from old York stone. Don't despair, for concrete is an ideal surface for the outdoor decorator to work on.

Suggested items: *paving slabs, molded stepping stones.*

Suitable finishes: *marbling, sandstone effect, verdigris effect, weathered-lead effect, weathered-terra-cotta effect.*

Plastic in the garden has many advantages over other materials; it is lightweight and can be molded into all manner of shapes and, unlike untreated metal, will not rust. The major disadvantage, however, is that plastic never develops any character of its own. Yet you can easily transform plastic garden items into treasures that evoke the test of time.

Suggested items: *planters, classical-shaped urns, molded wall features.*

Suitable finishes: *craquelure (works best on small items), marbling, patinating, rust effect, sandstone effect, verdigris effect, weathered-lead effect, weathered-terra-cotta effect.*

GETTING STARTED

Preparing Surfaces

Most new materials need little in the way of preparation. Older items may need to have old paint, varnish or rust removed before painting. Always make sure items are grease and dust free before being painted.

Commercial paint stripper, applied with an old paintbrush while wearing protective gloves, will bubble up and soften old paint or varnish on wood. Use steel wool or a scraper to rub it off.

Mineral spirits should be used instead of water to clean unpainted wood.

Scrapers and a wire brush will remove flaky paint from old wood and rust from metal.

Steel wool (1) is available in different grades. Use with mineral spirits to clean unpainted wood or on its own to rub back rusty metal. Coarse steel wool is also used for distressing paint while the finest steel wool is excellent for producing a really rich patina finish, and for applying polishing waxes. Wear protective gloves and a face mask when using steel wool.

Metal primers (2, 6) are designed for use with ferrous (iron) or non-ferrous surfaces and are available in spray and brush-on forms. Red oxide primer should be used on already rusted ferrous metal, while a multipurpose metal primer can be used on non-ferrous metals like galvanized metal, stainless steel and chrome. Always brush off loose rust before priming.

Universal primers (3) should be checked before they are bought. It is difficult for paint to adhere to plastics and other shiny materials, so buy a primer that is designed for hard-to-prime surfaces. Porous surfaces, like stone or terracotta, may need to be primed if you are covering them with something other than masonry paint.

Sandpaper (4) is available in different grades, the coarser it is, the more it will cut into your surface. Use sandpaper in the initial stages to smooth a rough surface or create a "key" in shiny paint for a new paint coat to adhere to. Wrap sandpaper around a wooden block for ease of use. Wear protective gloves and a face mask when sanding.

Wet-and-dry sandpaper (5) is less likely to scratch than ordinary sandpaper and does not create dust. Either wet the paper or dampen the surface before sanding. Wipe the sanded surface with a damp cloth occasionally.

Tack cloth (7) has a slightly sticky surface that is invaluable for picking up loose dust after sanding.

Quick-drying wood preservative (8) protects bare wood from rot. Do not use a creosote-based preservative under paint.

Stain-killing primer (9) seals unpainted wood and prevents sap seeping through the completed paint finish. Apply to knots with a paintbrush.

Rust-inhibiting primer and metal undercoats can be used to treat iron or steel that has already had loose rust brushed away, to prevent rust returning.

Some useful materials for surface preparation.

Brushes, Sponges and Rollers

Most of the brushes you need for outdoor paint effects are available from DIY stores.

General-purpose paintbrushes (1), in a variety of widths, have reasonably firm bristles.

Wire brushes (2) are essential for opening the grain in wood prior to liming.

Angled fitch brushes (3) are often made of hog hair, but synthetic varieties are available. They come in varying sizes and are used for marbling, spattering and freehand painting.

Varnish brushes (4) are flat and flexible and used to apply any kind of varnish.

Foam brushes (5), in a variety of widths, are useful for applying patinating solutions.

Softening brushes (6) are often made from badger or hog hair (badger is softer and more expensive) but synthetic varieties are available. Brush lightly over oil glaze to break up the original brushmarks.

Natural sea sponges (7) are essential for creating the texture of stone finishes.

Small rollers (8) are used to apply paint to a stamp.

Artists' brushes (9), made from synthetic or natural bristle, are available in a variety of sizes and are used for freehand painting.

Soft gilding brushes (10) are often made from badger hair, but synthetic varieties are available. Exceptionally soft, they are used to dust metallic powders over gold size, or to brush off loose pieces of metal leaf.

Round-headed fitch brushes (11) are excellent for stippling paint or glaze.

A selection of brushes, rollers and sponges used to create outdoor paint effects.

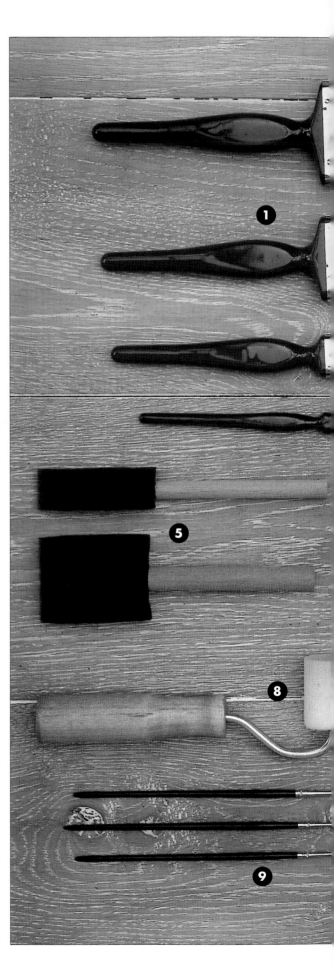

Types of Paint

There is a vast range of paints available, and some specific types are suitable for particular projects. There are thousands of colors to choose from, but you can also create your own shades by tinting paints yourself.

Oil-based paints are available in several finishes from dead flat, which gives a very matt finish, through to the mid-sheen finish of eggshell and the high sheen of gloss. Oil-based paints are slow drying and all can be sanded in between coats for a smooth finish. Use mineral spirits as a thinner and solvent. To tint your own oil-based paints, add artists' oil color.

Metallic paints in a smooth or hammered (beaten) finish, are specifically made for use over metal and require a special thinner. There are newer acrylic varieties available which, with the correct primer and sealer, can be used on any paintable surface.

Water-based paints are available in a number of forms. *Latex paint* is the most well known and is predominantly used for indoor projects. Latex is available in matte, a flat, chalky finish which remains porous, and satin, a mid-sheen finish that can be wiped clean easily. Water thinnable, latex is also quick drying. The range of premixed colors is vast, but to mix your own tint a base latex with artists' acrylic color.

Specialty thick matte latex has a chalky finish that makes it ideal for rubbing back with steel wool and can be found in specialty paint shops. Apply over preservative-treated wood for outdoor use.

Masonry or *wall paint* is specially prepared for outdoor use and comes in smooth and textured finishes. It is tougher and longer-lasting than latex and can be

Oil-based (1), metallic (2) and water-based paints (3) are available in many forms and finishes, suitable for indoor and outdoor use.

used on brickwork, concrete, cement, stone, terra-cotta and suitably primed plastic. Water thinnable, this paint is also quick drying. The range of premixed colors available is more limited than with latex, but you can tint masonry paint with artists' acrylic color. It is also possible to buy an additive which makes indoor latex suitable for exterior use.

Exterior wood paint is especially formulated to be water-repellent and to resist cracking and peeling. It can be used directly on rough or planed exterior wood, and the colors are fade resistant.

Stamping paint is designed specifically for stamping and is very quick drying.

Water-based paints are not suitable for direct use on a metal surface as they will eventually eat through the metal.

Gilding and Antiquing

Gilding and antiquing products are readily available and easy to use.

There is a wonderful range of products on the market that lets you produce special effects or an antique look easily and quickly.

Metallic powders (1) are available in a range of colors as well as the traditional gold, bronze, copper, silver and pewter. They are applied over tacky gold size.

Metal leaf (2) produces a wonderfully shiny finish. The wafer-thin sheets are available in real gold and silver or in the less expensive, but equally attractive, imitation forms of Dutch metal or brass (imitation gold) and aluminium (imitation silver), as well as copper. Sheets of transfer leaf are backed with fine paper that makes them easy to handle. Metal leaf is applied over tacky gold size and must be protected with special pale French polish (see page 18) to prevent tarnishing through oxidation.

Gilding wax (3) is rubbed on with a cloth or steel wool to produce a soft metallic finish and is available pretinted in a variety of metallic shades. Clean with mineral spirits.

Sparkle dust (4) is made up of tiny multicolored sparkling particles. Mix the dust with varnish to make a paint.

Liquidgems (5) are available in a range of jewel colors. They can be used alone or mixed with acrylic varnish.

Antiquing wax (6) is available tinted – usually in dark shades – or untinted. Apply it with a cloth or fine-grade steel wool to suggest an antique patina. Polish to create a velvety smooth finish. Clean with mineral spirits.

Oil-based (Japan) gold size (7) is a special glue used to adhere transfer metal leaf and metallic powders.

Antiquing patinas (8) come in liquid and cream form. Tinted in deep shades, they are applied with a cloth to give a worn look.

Glazes, Varnishes and Specialty Products

Glazes are transparent mediums to which color is added. When painted onto a surface they produce a translucent finish that dries reasonably slowly, giving you time to manipulate the glaze with a brush, rag or sponge to make a textured finish that reveals the base coat in places.

Harsh weather conditions can quickly erode paint and decorative finishes, so your projects need to be finished with a varnish that provides strong protection against frost and other elements.

Most of these glazes and varnishes can be bought in a DIY store; the specialty products are available from art supply stores.

Craquelure (1) is a specialty two-part water-based system that produces a crackled varnish effect.

Oil-based varnishes, also known as solvent-based varnishes, are available in a variety of forms and are very hard-wearing. They are slow drying and can be quite yellow in color. *Clear outdoor oil-based* varnish is available in a satin or high-gloss finish. Clean up and thin with mineral spirits and tint with artists' oil color.

Extra pale varnishes (2) are clear, refined varnishes used by professionals. They are not as yellow as other oil-based varnishes, so cause less alteration to the decoration beneath. Available in a dead flat or eggshell finish, this varnish is not especially produced for outdoor use, so you need to use several coats for absolute protection.

Polyurethane varnishes (3) are spirit-based, available in satin or gloss finishes and are ideal for outdoor use.

French polishes are made from shellac resin and are available in a range of colors. The palest, known as *special pale French polish* (4) is colorless, transparent and ideal for protecting a gilded surface from oxidation. *White polish* is a bleached version of French polish and is milky white in appearance, making it useful for sealing limed wood surfaces. For outdoor use I often apply a polyurethane varnish over the top for added protection.

Acrylic varnishes (5) are quick drying and water-solvent. Milky in initial appearance, they dry completely clear. They are not as durable as oil-based varnishes for exterior use. Acrylic varnishes can be tinted with

artists' acrylic color and are available in flat, satin or gloss finishes.

Acrylic glaze (6) is water-based, water-solvent and low-odor. It can be tinted any color with water-based media.

Whiting powder (7) is ground and refined calcium carbonate powder that is invaluable when creating a chalky or crusty weathered effect.

Crackle glaze (8) not to be confused with craquelure and also known as peeling-paint medium, is a water-based medium applied between two contrasting coats of water-based paint. As the top coat dries, cracks of varying sizes appear in the paint.

Acrylic texture gel (9) is available in a variety of different grades to create anything from a sand effect to a very coarse, rough look.

Oil glaze (10) is oil-based, mineral spirit-solvent and has quite a strong odor. It is slower drying than acrylic glaze – which means that it may pick up fibers and dust from the air as it dries. It can be tinted with any oil-based paint or color. Take great care when working with oil glaze since any material soaked in it is highly flammable. Always leave used rags to dry in a safe place and never put them in a pocket or bag.

THE PROJECTS

CHIPPED-PAINT EFFECT GARDEN SHED

Garden sheds usually live a forlorn, wallflower existence, either tucked away at the bottom of the garden or hidden behind a garage. Now, however, with the help of some of the new breed of exterior wood paints available in a range of glorious colors, the humble garden shed can be revived, taking on a new identity as a feature of the garden.

Materials and equipment

Wooden shed
Spray multipurpose metal primer
Blue spray metal paint
Cleaning brush
3 general-purpose paintbrushes
Clear quick-drying wood preservative (non-creosote based)
Forget-me-not blue water-based exterior wood paint
2 wooden or plastic sticks (chopsticks, for example)
Acrylic release wax
Lavender water-based exterior wood paint
Cotton cloth

This chipped-paint effect is easily achieved by using an acrylic release wax in between two coats of different-colored paint.

The door has been given the same treatment as the rest of the shed, but, for variety, the two paint colors have been reversed.

CHIPPED-PAINT FINISH

Using this two-color chipped-paint effect you can recreate the look of old, well-used wood that has been painted many times. A special acrylic release wax is sandwiched between two different-colored paints, then rubbed away when the top coat is dry. Use subdued colors that blend in with the surroundings, or, for a bold effect that draws attention to the painted wood, use strongly contrasting and bright paint colors. Using water-based paints which have been created especially for exterior wood not only revives the wood with color, but helps to preserve and weatherproof it as well.

PREPARATION

Before you start painting the shed, remove one hinge. Coat it with a spray multipurpose metal primer and leave to dry. Spray on a coat of blue metal paint. When dry, replace the hinge, remove the next hinge and repeat the process one by one until all the hinges, and the lock, are painted.

Remove dust and dirt from the exterior wood using a dry cleaning brush. Apply a coat of clear quick-drying wood preservative to all wood surfaces and allow to dry overnight.

ALTERNATIVE
For a subtle, more traditional feel which blends in with surrounding greenery, sandwich the release wax between two shades of green paint.

1 Working in the direction of the grain, use a paintbrush to apply a coat of forget-me-not blue water-based exterior wood paint to the horizontal slats of the shed, leaving out the door. Allow the first coat to dry before applying a second coat. Leave to dry.

4 Working in the direction of the grain again, apply a coat of lavender water-based exterior wood paint over the forget-me-knot blue base coat, covering the raised patches of acrylic release wax. Allow to dry overnight, then apply a second coat. Leave to dry.

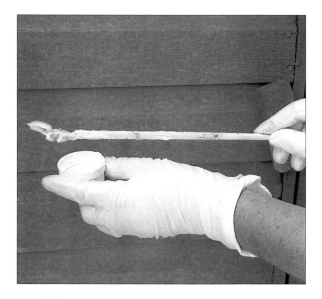

 Stir the acrylic release wax with a wooden or plastic stick. Use a clean stick to apply thickish blobs of wax in random patches over the base coat, varying their shape and size. Concentrate these patches on the edges and around the hinges and lock, the areas where paint would naturally get knocked and chip. Allow to dry.

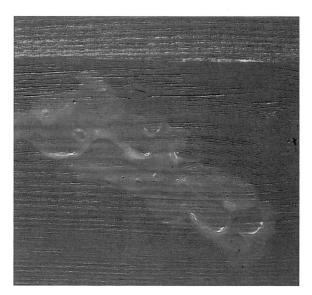

 When it is completely dry, the soft-textured, creamy-white acrylic release wax sets, becomes semi-transparent and takes on a slightly rubbery look and feel.

 Rub a damp cotton cloth over the raised release wax patches, revealing the color beneath, as if the top paint coat has naturally chipped in places. Some pressure may be needed, but persevere to achieve the full effect. Repeat the whole technique on the door, but reverse the colors so that lavender is revealed beneath chipped patches of forget-me-not blue.

GLAZING AND STAINING A GARDEN BENCH

This garden bench has been repainted on a number of occasions, which means that much of the intricate molding has become filled up with paint. Using tinted oil glaze and a combination of ragging and stippling techniques, these "lost" areas can be highlighted, giving them depth and character, while the wooden seat has a simple and complementary finish.

Materials and equipment

3 general-purpose paintbrushes
Metal primer (red oxide for ferrous metal or
    multipurpose for non-ferrous metal)
Undercoat for metal
Mid-green eggshell oil-based paint
Deep green eggshell oil-based paint
Oil glaze
Mineral spirits
Round-headed paintbrush
Cotton cloth
Softening brush
Gold ocher artists' oil color
Pointed-bristle brush
Varnish brush
Satin polyurethane varnish

FOR THE WOODEN SEAT
Cotton cloth
Mineral spirits
Sandpaper
3 general-purpose paintbrushes
Clear quick-drying wood preservative
    (non-creosote based)
Deep gold acrylic wood stain
Greyed-black water-based exterior wood paint

Caution
**Cloths used with oil glaze are highly
combustible while wet. Leave the cloth to dry
in a well-ventilated area before disposing of it.**

GLAZED AND STAINED FINISHES

To put the life and detail back into the metal frame, two traditional tinted oil glazes are mixed and applied. The main, deep green oil glaze is manipulated with a crumpled rag and softened with a very soft brush. The molded areas are highlighted with a gold oil glaze which is stippled on with a pointed-bristle brush.

The wooden slatted seat is stained gold using an acrylic wood stain, then covered with a coat of greyed-black exterior wood paint. When the wet paint is wiped off in places with a cloth the base color is revealed.

PREPARATION

Apply a suitable primer to the metal frame. Let this dry before applying undercoat for metal. Paint with two coats of mid-green, eggshell oil-based paint, allowing the first coat to dry overnight before applying the second.

Clean the wooden seat with mineral spirits and sand the surface to a smooth finish. Apply a coat of clear quick-drying wood preservative and leave to dry.

A delicate gold stipple highlights the ornamental flowers in the bench's metal frame.

In a clean glass jar, mix a colored oil glaze to a creamy consistency using equal amounts of deep green eggshell oil-based paint and oil glaze, and a little mineral spirits. Stir with a stick or shake well with the lid tightly on.

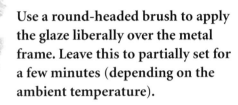
Use a round-headed brush to apply the glaze liberally over the metal frame. Leave this to partially set for a few minutes (depending on the ambient temperature).

Take a pad of clean, cotton cloth and gently pat and roll it over the still-wet glaze to create a texture.

Lightly brush a softening brush over the still-damp surface to soften harsh areas and create deeper pools of color. Leave to dry overnight.

5 Mix gold ocher artists' oil color, oil glaze and a little mineral spirits to a creamy consistency. Use a pointed-bristle brush to dab the gold glaze onto the ornamental motifs to highlight them. Soften with a scrunched-up cotton cloth. When dry, use a varnish brush to apply a coat of satin polyurethane varnish.

6 Load a paintbrush with a generous amount of deep gold acrylic wood stain and cover the wooden bench seat with a generous coat.

7 While the stain is still wet, wipe over the surface with a piece of clean cotton cloth. Allow to dry overnight.

8 Apply a light coat of greyed-black water-based exterior wood paint. Before this dries, wipe over the surface with a piece of clean cotton cloth to reduce the density of the dark color, allowing the deep gold to show through in places.

LIMING AND RUST EFFECT GARDEN TABLE

I persuaded my husband to make this sturdy hardwood table using oak planks as a top and the stand from an old sewing machine as a base. The top was limed, producing a characteristic chalky-white effect that enhances the natural grain of wood. I then chose to accentuate the aged feel of the base by giving it a rusted finish. The metal chairs were simply sprayed with blue paint for metal.

Materials and equipment

FOR THE WOODEN TABLETOP
4 general-purpose paintbrushes
Paint stripper
Soap and water
Clear quick-drying wood preservative (non-creosote based)
Wire brush
Tack cloth
Apron and protective gloves
Water-based liming paste
Medium-grade steel wool
3 varnish brushes
White polish
Satin polyurethane varnish
Extra pale eggshell oil-based varnish (optional)
Mineral spirits for cleaning varnish brushes

FOR THE METAL BASE
Wire brush
2 general-purpose paintbrushes
Metal primer (red oxide for ferrous metal or multipurpose for non-ferrous metal)
Silver spray paint for metal
Old general-purpose paintbrush
Instant Iron™ solution
Foam brush
Instant Rust™ solution
Varnish brush
Acrylic sealer

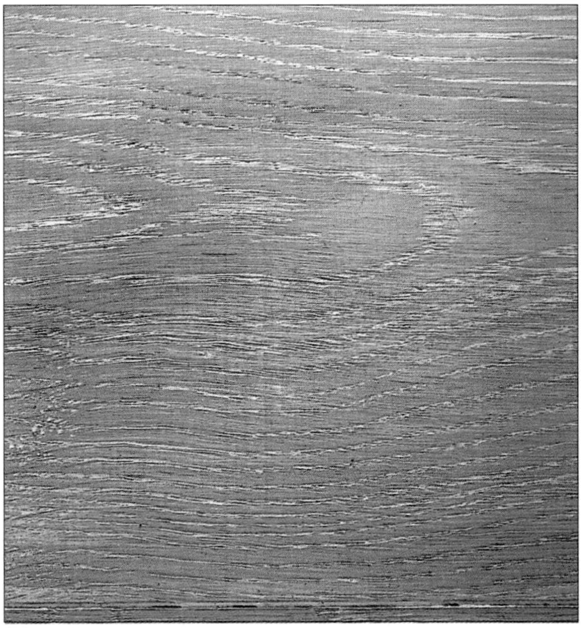

LIMED AND RUSTED FINISHES

Liming is an excellent technique for any hardwood with a good natural grain that can be opened with a wire brush. In this project, traditional liming wax has been replaced with a non-caustic, water-based liming paste which, unlike older products, can be sealed with varnish. The opened grain is painted with the paste and left to dry. Steel wool is then used to remove the surface paste, leaving the pores of the wood filled with the white residue. This process creates a lot of dust, so make sure you wear an apron and protective gloves. Working outside is ideal, but not on a windy day.

To complement the limed top, the metal base has been treated with a two-part system that creates an instant rust effect.

PREPARATION

Liming paste must be applied to bare wood surfaces, so strip and clean old, varnished or painted wood and neutralize the surface with soap and water. Allow the wood to dry, then apply a coat of clear quick-drying wood preservative to both sides of the tabletop and leave to dry for two to three days.

Remove loose rust and dirt from the metal base with a stiff wire brush. Prime with the relevant metal primer and leave to dry. Spray with silver paint for metal and allow to dry.

The natural grain of oak is beautifully emphasized by the use of white liming paste, a modern, water-based product that imitates the effects of traditional white wax.

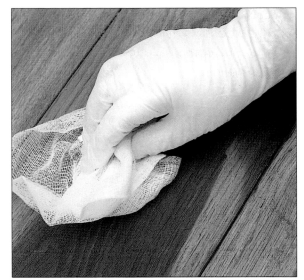

1 Work on a small section at a time. Use a paintbrush to brush water over the surface of the wood to dampen it. To open the grain, work a wire brush over the surface, always following the direction of the grain. Some pressure is needed.

2 Brush the dust off the surface and wipe with a tack cloth to remove all loose particles. Repeat across the whole surface.

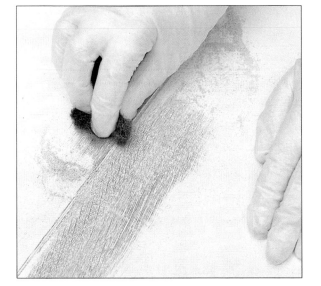

3 Wearing an apron and protective gloves, use a general-purpose paintbrush to apply the liming paste. To make sure you fill all the open pores of the wood, apply the paste in two directions – first follow the grain of the wood, then work across the grain. Let the liming paste dry completely.

4 Rub some medium-grade steel wool over the surface in the direction of the grain to remove excess liming paste. Do not use too much pressure as you may cut through the grain.

5 Use a varnish brush to apply a coat of white polish. This shellac-based varnish prevents the liming paste from being pulled out of the grain by the next coat of varnish. When dry, apply at least two coats of satin polyurethane varnish, letting each coat dry before applying the next. If you prefer to reduce the shine of the satin varnish, apply a coat of extra pale eggshell oil-based varnish. Do not forget to varnish the underside of the tabletop as well.

6 To give the metal base a rusted look, first shake the bottle of Instant Iron™ well. Use an old paintbrush to apply the first coat. Leave to dry for one hour, then apply a second coat. Let dry for 12 hours.

ALTERNATIVE
You could also try liming over wood that has been washed with a color. To make a wood wash, mix together equal parts of colored matte water-based exterior wood paint and water. Open the grain as usual and then apply the wood wash, brushing it over the surface in the direction of the grain. Before it dries, wipe over the surface with a dry cloth. Allow to dry before applying the liming paste.

7 Use a foam brush to apply a coat of Instant Rust™. Patches of rust will appear over the next few hours. Apply a second coat for a deeper color. When dry, apply a coat of acrylic sealer.

GILDING AND PATINATING A METAL GATE

This pretty garden gate, with its delicate leaves and stems, was found languishing at the back of a greenhouse. I gave it a new lease on life with a gilded effect using metallic powders. The gate is now used as a wall decoration, and provides the perfect backdrop for a display of trailing foliage and greenery.

Materials and equipment
Ornamental metal gate
Wire brush
Scraper
General-purpose paintbrush
Metal primer (red oxide for ferrous metal or multipurpose for non-ferrous metal)
Paper
3 narrow general-purpose paintbrushes
Blue eggshell oil-based paint
Blue-green eggshell oil-based paint
Narrow varnish brush
Oil-based gold size
Soft gilding brush
Copper metallic powder
Silver metallic powder
Special pale French polish
Denatured alcohol
Raw umber artists' oil color
Cotton cloth
Varnish brush
Satin polyurethane varnish
Mineral spirits for cleaning varnish brushes

Caution
Always work in a well-ventilated area when using denatured alcohol.

The copper metallic powder adds a pink tinge to the blue-green base coat, while the silver powder lightens the background color.

PATINATED GILDING FINISH

This alternative method of gilding uses metallic powders instead of the more traditional metal leaf. When the powders are used sparingly, glimpses of the blue and blue-green base coat can still be seen, as if the metallic finish is translucent. A final coat of tinted French polish, dabbed with a rag, slightly dulls and ages the metallic powders, adding a further dimension.

PREPARATION

Remove all loose rust and dirt using a wire brush and scraper. Either brush on or spray the metal with two coats of the appropriate primer. Allow the first coat to thoroughly dry before applying the second. Leave to dry.

1 Work on a flat surface over a sheet of paper: this will enable you to keep the excess metallic powder. Using narrow paintbrushes, randomly apply both the blue and blue-green eggshell oil-based paints, overlapping the colors in places. Leave to dry overnight.

4 To age the gilding, mix some special pale French polish with an equal amount of denatured alcohol, and tint with a little raw umber artists' oil color. Paint this mix generously over the gilded areas of the gate.

ALTERNATIVE
You can also use colored metallic powders instead of copper and silver. For example, try emerald green powder over a pale green base.

 Working in manageable sections, use a narrow varnish brush to apply a coat of oil-based gold size and leave until tacky.

Pour a small quantity of copper metallic powder into the lid of the jar. Pick up a little powder on a soft gilding brush and dust it over the gold size, without completely covering the base coat. Repeat with the silver powder, working randomly. Complete the whole gate in the same way, turning it over to reach all the painted areas. Leave for 24 hours to thoroughly adhere.

Dab the still-wet varnish with a pad of clean cotton cloth to create a randomly patinated effect. Leave to dry for 24 hours, then varnish with several coats of satin polyurethane varnish, allowing each coat to dry before applying the next.

CRACKLE GLAZE AND WAX RESIST ON A POTTING BENCH

This painted and aged potting bench provides the style-conscious gardener with a perfect place for stacking and storing all kinds of garden paraphernalia. Having started out as a rather ordinary, and obviously new, piece of outdoor furniture, the bench now has the look of a well-used and well-loved item, which has become weathered and distressed with age.

Materials and equipment

Wooden potting bench
5 general-purpose paintbrushes
Stain-killing primer
Clear quick-drying wood preservative (non-creosote based)
Sandpaper
Pale putty water-based exterior wood paint
Water-based crackle glaze (peeling-paint medium)
Candle
Greyed-green water-based exterior wood paint
Medium-grade steel wool
Cotton cloth
Green antiquing patina
Varnish brush
Extra pale dead flat oil-based varnish
Mineral spirits for cleaning varnish brush

This wonderful aging technique, which combines a modern commercial peeling-paint medium with candle wax and an antiquing patina, gives the look of old worn layers of paint, and is simple to achieve.

DISTRESSED-PAINT FINISH

The cracked paint look on this bench is achieved using a crackle glaze, also known as peeling-paint medium, sandwiched between two coats of water-based paint. Care must be taken when painting over the crackle glaze: it is important that you do not overbrush since this action will cause the crackle glaze layer to peel off.

A resist technique – using candle wax to stop the top coat of paint from adhering properly – is used in some areas for a distressed look, as if the paint has been rubbed away over the years due to plenty of use.

PREPARATION

Use a paintbrush to apply stain-killing primer to any knots in the wood and leave to dry. This will seal the knots and prevent any sap seeping through and spoiling the painted finish. Apply a coat of clear quick-drying wood preservative and allow to dry. Sand and smooth off any rough edges.

1 Using a paintbrush, apply a heavy coat of pale putty matte water-based exterior wood paint to all the surfaces. Leave for several hours to dry thoroughly.

4 Apply a generous coat of greyed-green water-based exterior wood paint all over, taking care not to overbrush the crackle glazed areas as this will pull the medium away. Leave to dry overnight.

ALTERNATIVES
To achieve a really aged look, apply crackle glaze all over the base coat and leave out the candle wax.
•
Or, for a more subtle look, use the candle wax without the crackle glaze.

Using a dry paintbrush, apply a few random patches of crackle glaze to the dry base coat, always working in the direction of the grain. Allow to dry thoroughly.

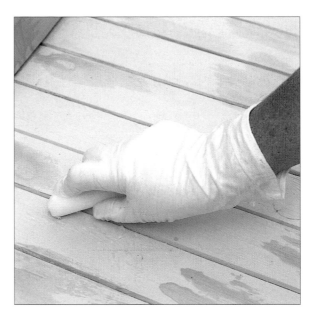

Rub the candle over other random areas of the base coat, particularly along the edges, avoiding the patches of crackle glaze. The candle wax does not have to be left to dry.

In those areas that were crackle glazed, the top coat of paint will have cracked, revealing the base coat. The areas rubbed with candle wax will show up as dark patches. Rub medium-grade steel wool into these patches to easily remove some of the paint.

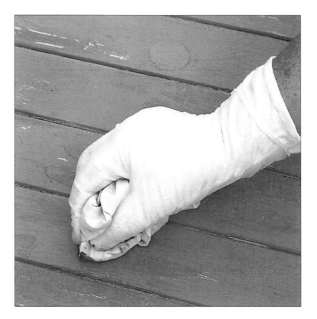

To age the piece further, use a cotton cloth to rub some green antiquing patina into the edges and corners. When the patina is dry, use a varnish brush to apply several coats of extra pale dead flat oil-based varnish, letting each coat dry before applying the next.

WEATHERED-LEAD EFFECT WALL FEATURE

It is hard to believe that this ornate lion's-head wall feature is made from plastic and not weathered lead. Decorated in this way, the wall feature would also look wonderful as a water feature, simply buy a pump kit from your local garden center.

Materials and equipment
Plastic wall feature
7 general-purpose paintbrushes
Universal primer (suitable for use on plastic)
Slate blue-grey smooth water-based
    masonry paint
Pewter metallic water-based paint
Ivory black artists' acrylic color
Acrylic glaze
Ultramarine artists' acrylic color
Matte acrylic varnish
Whiting powder
2 varnish brushes
Extra pale eggshell oil-based varnish
Satin polyurethane varnish
Mineral spirits for cleaning varnish brushes

By applying paints, glazes and whiting powder in vertical streaks you can produce a realistic weathered finish, making brand new plastic look like naturally aged metal.

WEATHERED-LEAD FINISH

This salty, blue-grey lead-effect finish is achieved by layering water-based masonry paint, tinted glazes, paint washes and whiting powder. To produce a realistic weathered effect, as if the mask has been in position on a wall for many years, hold it vertically while working. The paint and washes trickle down the mask to make downward streaks that imitate the effects of the elements.

PREPARATION

Apply a coat of universal primer and leave to dry. Apply a second coat and let dry. Apply a base coat of slate blue-grey smooth water-based masonry paint. Allow to dry.

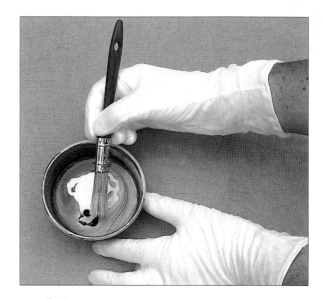

Blacken some pewter metallic water-based paint with a little ivory black artists' acrylic color, then add a small amount of acrylic glaze to make a creamy consistency.

Continuing with the mask held vertically, randomly apply some slate blue-grey masonry paint. Again, take the damp paintbrush and wash the still-wet paint downward over the mask, building up the streaky look. Allow to dry.

Add some ultramarine and ivory black artists' acrylic color to the slate blue-grey masonry paint to darken it. Paint random downward streaks of this deeper color and wash through again with the damp brush. Allow to dry.

Use a paintbrush to apply the glaze to the mask, covering it randomly but thoroughly and working the color well into the crevices.

Before the glaze coat dries, hold the mask vertically and pull a damp paintbrush over it from top to bottom, to create a slightly streaky look. Allow to dry.

Use a paintbrush to apply vertical streaks of matte acrylic varnish, pushing the varnish into random crevices. Trickle some whiting powder over the varnished areas. Using the same brush, carefully wash the whiting powder over the mask, particularly into the ornamental areas, to produce a salt-weathered look. Leave to dry overnight. Protect with two coats of extra pale eggshell oil-based varnish and a coat of satin polyurethane varnish, letting each coat dry before applying the next.

ALTERNATIVE
You can increase the weathered look by layering even more wash coats. Continue varying the shade of blue-grey by adding more ivory and ultramarine.

MARBLING A PLASTER COLUMN

This plaster column has been transformed into a stylish ornament using a fantasy marble finish. The pale pink marble created here is cool and sophisticated, the perfect foil for a trailing ivy.

Materials and equipment

Plaster column
2 general-purpose paintbrushes
Universal primer (suitable for use on plaster)
White eggshell oil-based paint
Natural sea sponge
Mineral spirits
Oil glaze
Cotton cloth
Burnt umber artists' oil color
White artists' oil color
Fine artists' brush
Varnish brush
Satin polyurethane varnish

Caution

Sponges and cloths used with oil glaze are highly combustible while wet. Never put a sponge or cloth that has been in contact with oil glaze in a bag or pocket. Leave it to dry in a well-ventilated area before disposing of it.

A marbled effect can be applied to a multitude of garden ornaments. In the following steps a plaster column is given a fantasy marble finish, while the obelisk pictured on the left has been greatly enhanced by a painted sienna marble.

MARBLE FINISH

Marble is a very special stone that is out of reach for many people's pockets. So why not produce a fantasy marble? Oil-based glaze, tinted with artists' oil colors and thinned with mineral spirits, is sponged onto the surface and painted on with a fine artists' brush to produce veins. For the most realistic end result, study photographs of real marble to see how the veining looks, and use closely toned colors for an authentic finish. The final varnish coats are very important as they add depth to the effect.

PREPARATION

Paint the column with two coats of universal primer, letting the first coat dry completely before applying the second. Apply two coats of white eggshell oil-based paint, allowing each coat to dry before applying the next. Prepare the sponge for use by soaking it in water then squeezing it out as dry as possible. Dip it in a little mineral spirits and squeeze the excess out again.

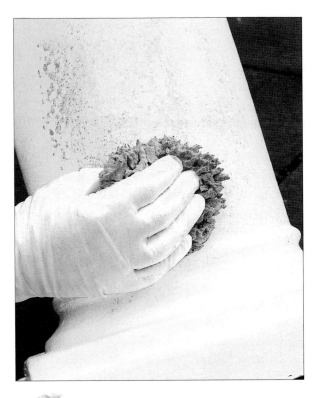

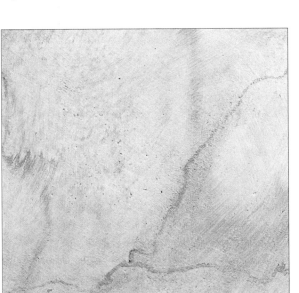

1 Make up a light pinky glaze using oil glaze and a little mineral spirits tinted with burnt umber and white artists' oil color. The mix should be like thin cream, but not too runny. Using the prepared sponge, apply the glaze all over the column, building up the color in some areas and reducing it in others to create variation.

"Faux", or fantasy marble is only intended to create an illusion of the real thing, so this is a finish that you can have real fun with. You will find that the smoother the original surface the better the final result will be.

ALTERNATIVES
If your project is going to be kept in a conservatory, or protected from outdoor conditions, you could use a water-based base coat, an acrylic glaze and artists' acrylic colors, followed by several coats of acrylic varnish.

•

Use black and white oil colors to imitate grey marble, or raw sienna, burnt sienna and white oil colors to reproduce a sienna marble.

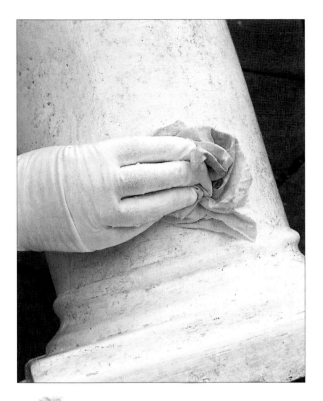

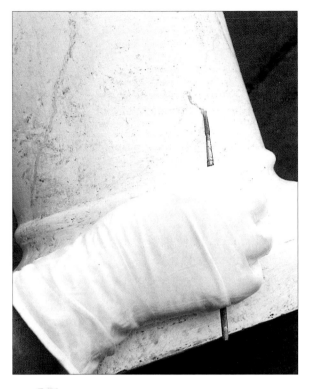

2 Take a pad of crumpled cotton cloth. Roll and dab the fabric over the still-wet glaze to create more texture. Re-form the cloth as it becomes saturated with glaze.

3 Squeeze a little burnt umber and white artists' oil color onto a flat container. Put a little oil glaze and mineral spirits in two other containers. Using a fine artists' brush, pick up small amounts of the two oil colors with just enough oil glaze and mineral spirits to make a thin mix. Now paint in veins of color, working vertically and diagonally. Vary the thickness and density of the veins, and the color slightly.

4 To make the veins appear less obvious and merge slightly into the background, gently stroke over the surface with a softening brush. Continue adding veins and softening the effect until you are happy with the overall look. Leave to dry before using a varnish brush to apply several coats of satin polyurethane varnish, letting each coat dry before applying the next.

VERDIGRIS EFFECT CONTAINER

Giving this inexpensive planter a "faux" finish has changed it beyond recognition. Now it has a weathered look that completely disguises the fact that it is plastic.

Materials and equipment

Square plastic planter with raised design
8 general-purpose paintbrushes
Universal primer (suitable for use on plastic)
Red-brown smooth water-based masonry paint
Antique gold metallic water-based paint
Bronze artists' acrylic color
Acrylic glaze
Blue-green smooth water-based masonry paint
White artists' acrylic color
Denatured alcohol
Whiting powder (sifted to remove lumps)
Yellow ocher artists' acrylic color
Bright green artists' acrylic color
2 varnish brushes
Satin polyurethane varnish
Extra pale dead flat varnish
Mineral spirits for cleaning varnish brushes

Caution
Always work in a well-ventilated area when using denatured alcohol.

Layering paint, denatured alcohol and whiting powder and letting them run vertically down the surface creates the verdigris look.

VERDIGRIS FINISH

The look of verdigris, a greenish deposit which forms naturally on copper or brass that has been exposed to the elements, can be imitated using water-based paints and glaze, whiting powder and denatured alcohol. The beauty of this technique is that you can control the intensity of color by varying the shades of the paints and glazes.

PREPARATION

Apply a coat of universal primer to the outside and part way down inside the planter. When dry, cover with a coat of red-brown smooth water-based masonry paint. Leave to dry overnight.

1 Darken some antique gold metallic water-based paint with a little bronze artists' acrylic color, then thin the mixture to the consistency of cream using a small amount of acrylic glaze. Use a paintbrush to roughly apply the glaze all over the prepared surface. Leave to dry.

2 Divide some blue-green smooth water-based masonry paint between two containers. Lighten one batch using a little white artists' acrylic color. Mix some denatured alcohol into both batches to achieve a thin, pourable consistency. Add enough sifted whiting powder to both batches to make thickish pastes. Use an old paintbrush to stipple or dab on the deeper paste mix in random patches over the surface.

3 Load a brush with a little denatured alcohol and stipple it onto the still-wet surface, letting the liquid also run downward off the brush.

4 While still damp, sprinkle whiting powder vertically over the surface and press it into the raised areas. Before the surface dries you can gently rub away some of the top coat to reveal the underlying colors.

Apply the lighter paste mix in the same way, stippling the color into the gaps left by the first paste.

Mix yellow ocher artists' acrylic color with water to make a thin wash. Load a paintbrush with the diluted paint and let it trickle down the surface, paying particular attention to the raised areas.

Mix a little bright green artists' acrylic color with some acrylic glaze until it is slowly pourable. Load a brush with the glaze and let it run down the container in rivulets. Leave for at least a day to dry thoroughly. Apply two coats of satin polyurethane varnish, letting the first coat dry overnight before applying the second. To reduce the shine, finish with a coat of extra pale dead flat oil-based varnish.

ALTERNATIVES

Other effective base coats are copper, gold or black.

•

Commercial patinating kits can also be used to produce a verdigris finish. The green patinating solution in the kit reacts with the metallic base coat to recreate the look.

PATINATING A GARDEN LANTERN

There is no need to rely on the light of the silvery moon to brighten your garden at night, garden lanterns can be bought in all shapes and sizes. This new lantern has been patinated to make it appear old, giving it a more interesting look.

Materials and equipment
Metal lantern
General-purpose paintbrush
3 small disposable bristle paintbrushes
Patinating system containing:
    Clear primer for metal
    Blackened bronze base coat
    Blue patina solution
    Burgundy aging tint
    Acrylic sealer
Varnish brush

PATINATED FINISH

This aged patina finish is achieved using commercial products created for just this purpose. These water-based systems enable you to age and weather new, characterless metal items with ease. While the patina used here gives a blue-green cast over a deep bronze base coat, the final aging tint develops into a white, crusty effect.

PREPARATION

Make sure the surface is clean and free from oil, grease and lacquer.

Water-based patinating kits, like the one used to age this garden lantern, are easy to use to add character to otherwise uninspiring pieces of garden furniture.

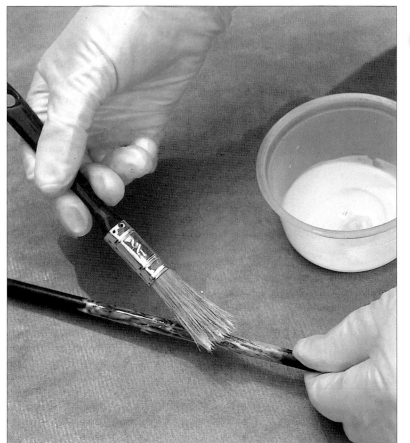

 Use a paintbrush to apply a coat of clear primer for metal included in the patinating system. Allow to dry. Apply a second coat and leave to dry for 12 hours.

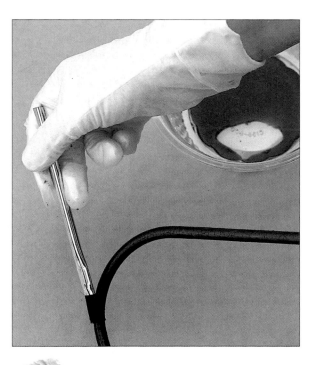

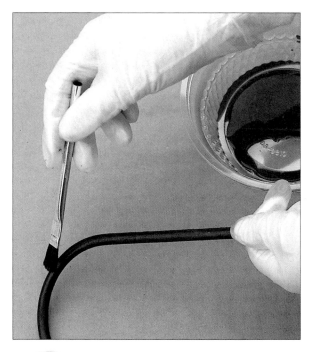

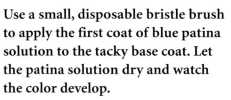 Use a small, disposable bristle brush to apply the first coat of blue patina solution to the tacky base coat. Let the patina solution dry and watch the color develop.

To enrich the color, reapply the blue patina solution and leave to thoroughly dry.

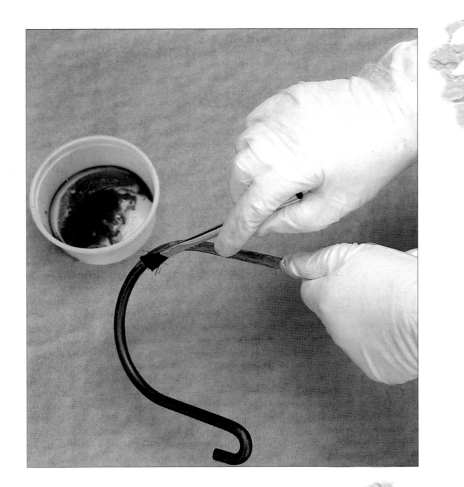

2 Shake the bottle of blackened bronze base coat well, ensuring the metal particles are evenly distributed. Use a small, disposable bristle paintbrush to apply the first coat. Allow to dry thoroughly. Apply a second coat of blackened bronze in the same way, but only let this dry until tacky – usually between three and eight minutes.

5 When you are happy with the depth of color, add further interest with some highlights. Mix a small amount of burgundy aging tint with some of the patina solution on a saucer. Use a small, disposable bristle brush to randomly apply the tint to areas of the piece. Allow to dry overnight. Protect the decoration with a coat of the acrylic sealer included in the kit.

ALTERNATIVE
Patinating systems using different color combinations are also available, so have a good look at what is in stock in your art supply store to decide which one you prefer.

SANDSTONE EFFECT ATHENIAN JAR

You could quite easily believe that this planter has stood for decades in the heat of the Mediterranean sunshine. Not so, for this container, which has been transformed with a sandstone finish, is very new and made of plastic, which means there is no danger of the frost damaging it or of it getting broken.

Materials and equipment
Ornamental plastic planter
General-purpose paintbrush
Universal primer (suitable for use on plastic)
2 angled fitch brushes
Coarse texture acrylic gel
Fine sand
Off-white smooth water-based masonry paint
Yellow ocher artists' acrylic color
Raw umber artists' acrylic color
Natural sea sponge
Paper towel
2 varnish brushes
Satin polyurethane varnish
Extra pale dead flat oil-based varnish
Mineral spirits for cleaning varnish brushes

By building up sponged layers of natural stone colors, and adding some texture, you can create an authentic-looking sandstone finish.

SANDSTONE FINISH

This technique relies largely upon the use of very natural shades of water-based paint, the texture of a sea sponge and the addition of some coarse textured acrylic gel and fine sand. The textured gel and sand are applied over the primer coat to create drifts of crustiness on the surface of the pot. Small amounts of water-based masonry paint, in a variety of shades of off-white, are dabbed on with a natural sea sponge to imitate the grainy look of stone.

PREPARATION

Paint a coat of universal primer all over the exterior and down about 3in (7.5cm) inside the pot. Allow to dry thoroughly.

Using an angled fitch brush, apply drifts of coarse texture acrylic gel to the outside of the pot, building up raised areas of texture.

Wash the sponge in clean water and squeeze it out as before. Sponge on some of the yellow ocher paint mix in drifts. Do not cover all the surface. Allow to dry.

Repeat Step 4 with the raw umber paint mix, filling in and around the yellow ocher effect. Add a little more raw umber to the paint mix and dab this on in places to increase the contrast slightly.

To add to the coarseness, sprinkle some fine sand over the still-wet textured gel.

Divide some off-white smooth water-based masonry paint between three shallow containers. Keep one in its natural state, add some yellow ocher artists' acrylic color to the second and some raw umber to the third, making slightly varying shades of off-white. Wet a natural sponge and squeeze it out until just damp. Dip it into the natural off-white paint, removing the excess on some paper towel. Use a pouncing action to apply the paint all over the pot, not forgetting the inside edge. Allow to dry.

Load an angled fitch brush with the deeper raw umber mix and run your fingers through the bristles to randomly spatter the paint on. Allow to dry. Use a varnish brush to apply a coat of satin polyurethane varnish. Let dry. For an authentic old stone look, apply a coat of extra pale dead flat oil-based varnish.

ALTERNATIVE
To reproduce a dark granite effect, substitute shades of off-white paint with shades of grey, ranging from pale grey to near black.

WEATHERED-TERRA-COTTA EFFECT STEPPING STONES

In their natural state, these molded concrete stepping stones provide a much-needed path, but lack any real character. Transform concrete by giving it a weathered-terra-cotta finish, building up a painted texture that resembles natural stone.

Materials and equipment

Concrete stepping stones
Stiff brush
3 general-purpose paintbrushes
Light stone smooth water-based masonry paint
Mid-stone smooth water-based masonry paint
Red-brown smooth water-based masonry paint
Natural sea sponge
Raw umber artists' acrylic color
Olive green smooth water-based masonry paint
Paper towel
White smooth water-based masonry paint
Whiting powder
Varnish brush
Extra pale dead flat oil-based varnish
Mineral spirits for cleaning varnish brush

WEATHERED-TERRA-COTTA FINISH

Natural terra-cotta has many shades, ranging from pale pinkish-brown to a deep red-brown. Age and weather can give it a green cast, from algae growing on it, or a white, dusty look that comes from the natural salts in the stone. This technique aims to recreate this rustic look, using several shades of water-based masonry paint, whiting powder and a natural sponge.

PREPARATION

Brush the concrete stones with a stiff brush to remove loose dirt and debris.

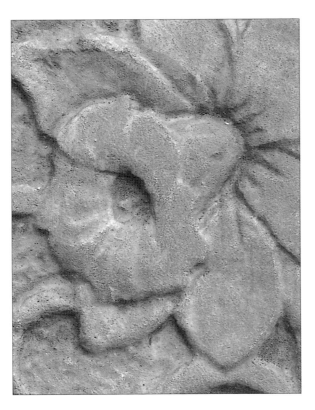

Diluted white masonry paint and some whiting powder gives the painted concrete stepping stone a chalky, weathered look.

1 Use a paintbrush to roughly cover the stone with one coat of light stone smooth water-based masonry paint, pushing the paint right into the molded areas. Allow to dry.

2 Roughly apply mid-stone water-based masonry paint to areas of the stone, building up variations in the overall texture to achieve the natural stone look. Allow to dry.

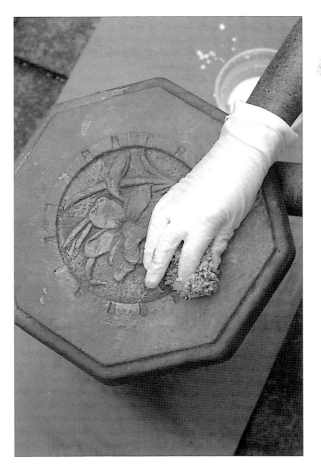

To produce a whitewash look, mix a little white smooth water-based masonry paint with enough water to make a creamy consistency. Rinse out the sponge and use it to dampen the surface of the stone. Dip the sponge in the whitewash. Hold the stone at an angle and squeeze out the sponge, letting the whitewash trickle over the surface. Allow to dry.

ALTERNATIVES

To increase the weathered look further, reapply the dulled green paint mixture to the raised design and repeat Steps 5 and 6.

•

This finish is also perfect for making a large plastic container look like its equivalent in real terra-cotta, which would be prohibitively expensive, and very heavy.

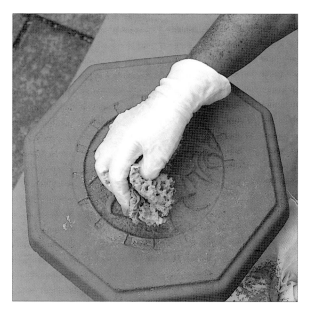

Roughly apply red-brown smooth water-based masonry paint in the same way, varying the application to build up texture. Allow to dry.

Dampen a natural sponge and squeeze out the excess water. Mix a little raw umber artists' acrylic color into a small amount of olive green smooth water-based masonry paint – just enough to dull the green. Dip the damp sponge into the mixture and blot it on some paper towel. Use a soft dabbing motion to apply the green to a few areas of the stone – just enough to suggest shading and the look of lichen.

Dampen the sponge again and use it to dab some more of the whitewash over the entire piece. Before this coat dries, take a little whiting powder and push it into the molded areas of the stone, accentuating the weathered, chalky look. Allow to dry before applying two coats of extra pale dead flat oil-based varnish to protect the finish without affecting the dusty look of natural terra-cotta. Let the first coat dry before applying the second.

TWO-TONE DRY-BRUSHING A PLANTER

The simple shape of this wooden planter inspired the two-color effect used to decorate it. The clean colors and rough paint application produce a finish that is both modern and stylish, yet soft and slightly worn.

Materials and equipment

Wooden planter
4 general-purpose paintbrushes
Stain-killing primer
Clear quick-drying wood preservative (non-creosote based)
Bright yellowed-green flat latex paint
Fine-grade steel wool
Swedish blue flat latex paint
Cotton rag
2 varnish brushes
Satin polyurethane varnish
Extra pale dead flat oil-based varnish
Mineral spirits for cleaning varnish brushes

DRY-BRUSHED FINISH

The top coat of paint in this two-tone finish looks as if it has been naturally worn over time. The base color is applied solidly over the planter, then burnished, when dry, with fine-grade steel wool to give a soft sheen. The contrasting top color is thinned slightly with water, then applied in the direction of the grain of the wood, leaving areas of the base coat uncovered. The secret of success with this technique lies in applying very little of the second color, just dip the tips of the bristles in the paint, and use your brush sideways to keep the application light and slightly random.

PREPARATION

Use a paintbrush to apply stain-killing primer to any knots in the wood. This will seal them and prevent sap seeping through and spoiling the painted finish. Allow to dry. Apply a coat of clear quick-drying wood preservative to all the surfaces and leave to dry for several days.

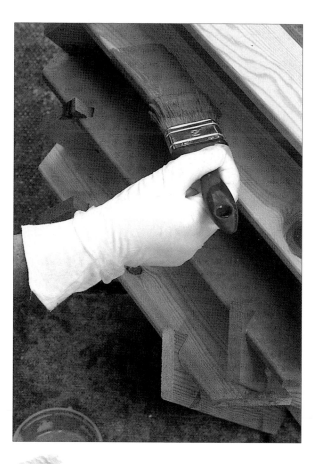

Use a paintbrush to apply a coat of bright yellowed-green flat latex paint, working in the direction of the grain. Leave to dry for several hours.

Applying a small amount of paint with a random flourish is the secret to making this finish look like naturally worn paint.

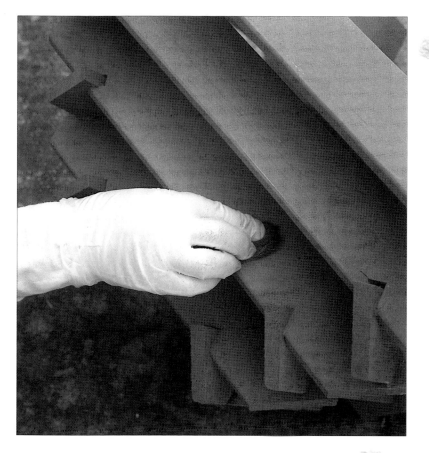

Burnish the paint lightly using fine-grade steel wool to give it a soft sheen.

Mix a wash of 3 parts Swedish blue flat latex paint to 1 part water. Dip the tips of the bristles of a paintbrush into the mix. Position the side of the brush on the surface and gently stroke it over the base color in the direction of the grain, leaving random areas uncovered. When nearly dry, wipe over the damp surface with a dry cotton cloth. Allow to dry. Burnish again using fine-grade steel wool. Use a varnish brush to apply two coats of satin polyurethane varnish, letting the first coat dry before applying the second. To dull the shine, finish with a coat of extra pale dead flat oil-based varnish.

ALTERNATIVE
Some other effective color combinations for this technique are grey and blue, pink and red or deep blue and light blue.

TWO-TONE DRY-BRUSHING

CRAQUELURE CLAY SPHERES

These ornamental spheres create an unusual feature in any garden, whether partially hidden among foliage or plants, or sitting proudly on top of a wall. Wherever you place them, the craquelure finish adds instant antiquity and an unexpected dimension.

Materials and equipment

Ornamental clay garden spheres
3 general-purpose paintbrushes
Universal primer (suitable for use on clay)
Bright blue smooth water-based masonry paint
Pewter metallic water-based paint
Copper metallic water-based paint
3 varnish brushes
Two-part acrylic craquelure system (base coat and top coat)
Cotton cloth
Raw umber artists' oil color
Mineral spirits
Satin polyurethane varnish

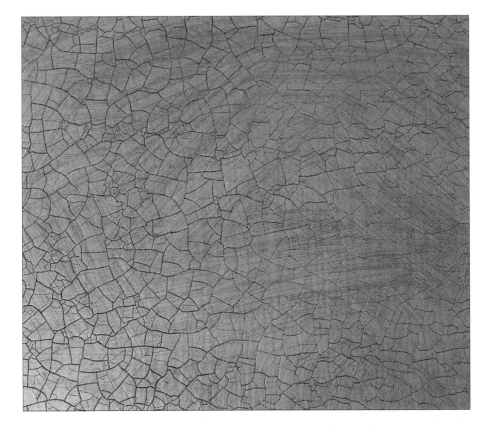

The two-part craquelure system, finished with some artists' oil color, enables you to imitate the network of fine cracks that appears with age in varnish, and to produce a remarkable antique finish.

CRAQUELURE FINISH

Craquelure is a notoriously temperamental finish to achieve, particularly using the older, oil-based products. The newer, and more environmentally friendly systems, are water-based, but work in the same way to produce an equally realistic effect. The base and top coat work against one another to create a network of fine cracks that are barely visible to the naked eye. However, once a dark artists' oil color or tinted wax has been rubbed in and the excess removed, the highlighted cracks are a magical sight.

PREPARATION

The two-part craquelure system will not work effectively on an absorbent surface, so, in order to reduce the porosity of the natural clay, first apply a coat of universal primer.

Use a paintbrush to apply a coat of bright blue smooth water-based masonry paint over the ball. Allow to dry overnight.

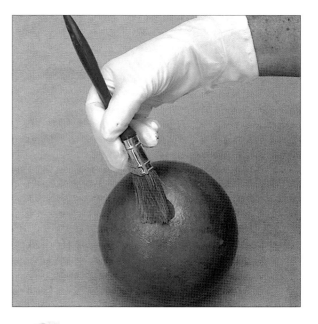

Using a slightly dampened varnish brush, carefully brush on a layer of the craquelure top coat. Try not to drag the brush over the surface since this may pull the base coat away. As the craquelure dries, cracks appear in the top varnish layer.

ALTERNATIVES
For a lighter effect, paint the primed clay ball with a coat of pale blue water-based masonry paint and apply the two coats of craquelure as before. Use a pewter wax to highlight the cracks and clean the surface with mineral spirits.

•

If you prefer, you can produce a network of much larger cracks by using the appropriate base coat, available as an alternative in most two-part craquelure systems.

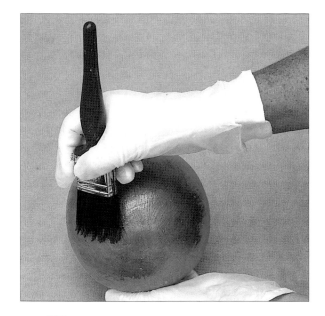

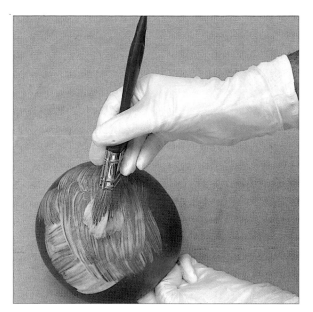

Brush on some pewter and copper metallic water-based paint, dragging and stippling the two colors so that they blend together but do not merge totally. Leave overnight to thoroughly dry .

Use a varnish brush to apply a generous coat of the craquelure base coat. Leave to dry, following the manufacturer's instructions to find out how long this will take.

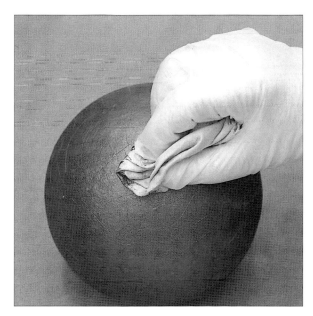

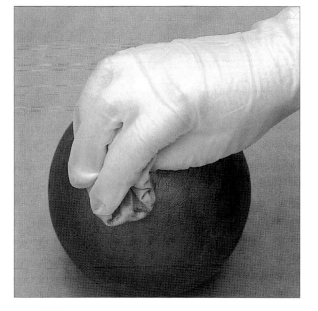

When completely dry, use a cotton cloth to rub raw umber artists' oil color over the surface, pushing it into the cracks. Dip a cloth in some mineral spirits and use this to remove the excess oil paint from the surface of the ball, leaving the color in the cracks only.

Buff the surface with a dry cloth. Seal with two coats of satin polyurethane varnish, allowing the first coat to dry before applying the second.

METAL LEAF WINDOW TROUGH

Galvanized metal containers have undergone a revival of late and make excellent outdoor containers. This window trough was transformed into a lasting treasure using a mix of copper and imitation gold transfer metal leaf.

Materials and equipment
Galvanized metal trough
2 general-purpose paintbrushes
Multipurpose metal primer for non-ferrous metal
Blackboard paint
3 varnish brushes
Oil-based gold size
Copper transfer leaf
Dutch metal (imitation gold) transfer leaf
Soft cloth
Soft gilding brush
Special pale French polish
Satin polyurethane varnish
Mineral spirits for cleaning varnish brushes

Imitation gold leaf is cheaper than the real thing but I doubt that anybody who sees this trough will be able to tell the difference.

METAL LEAF FINISH

Metal leaf provides the shiniest metallic finish imaginable, and a final gentle polishing with a soft cloth accentuates that quality. Gilding with transfer leaf does take some practice, so try the technique on a hidden surface first. As this is an outdoor project, I have used oil-based (Japan) gold size, which is left to become tacky before the transfer leaf is applied.

PREPARATION

Ensure the surface is free from grease and dirt. Apply metal primer to the outside and down about 2in (5cm) inside the trough. Leave to dry before applying a second coat.

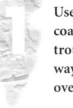 Use a paintbrush to apply an even coat of blackboard paint to the trough, not forgetting to go part way down inside it. Allow to dry overnight.

 Use a varnish brush to apply a thin coat of oil-based gold size, brushing out any air bubbles. Wait for the size to become tacky but not dry: on a hot day the drying time will be quite quick so it is a good idea to work on small areas at a time.

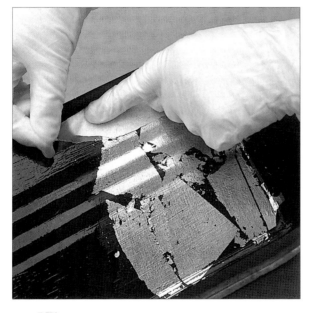

Repeat Step 3 to fill in the gaps with Dutch metal transfer leaf. Use small pieces of excess leaf in copper or Dutch metal to fill the smaller gaps.

Brush gently over the trough with a soft gilding brush to remove any loose leaf. Rub very gently over the leaf with a soft cloth to create a sheen. Continue to gild the whole trough in the same way.

3 Take a sheet of copper transfer leaf and, while the protective backing paper is still attached, tear off an uneven shape. Press the leaf against the tacky size and gently rub the backing paper. As the leaf adheres the paper will become loose and can be peeled away. Apply more torn copper leaf over the trough, leaving random gaps of varying sizes.

6 Protect the gilded object with a coat of special pale French polish. This will prevent the Dutch metal leaf tarnishing and turning black. For further outdoor protection, apply several coats of satin polyurethane varnish, letting each coat dry completely before applying the next.

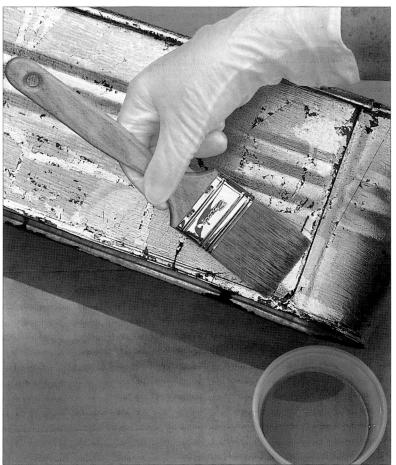

COLOR WASHING AND WAXING A PEG RAIL

This sturdy, functional item, with its shelf for storing pots and hooks for hanging garden tools, has been given a no-nonsense, color-wash and wax finish that complements its practical design.

A thin wash of diluted latex paint, some tinted wax and a quick buff with fine-grade steel wool is all that is needed to emphasize the grain of this wooden peg rail.

Materials and equipment

Peg rail
Sandpaper
Tack cloth
4 general-purpose paintbrushes
Clear quick-drying wood preservative (non-creosote based)
Red flat latex paint
Cotton cloth
Yellow flat latex paint
Red-tinted wax
Fine-grade steel wool
Varnish brush
Extra pale dead flat oil-based varnish
Mineral spirits for cleaning varnish brush

COLOR-WASH AND WAX FINISH

This is a brilliant finish that enhances and colors the natural grain of untreated wood, emphasizing the inherent beauty of the timber. Simply brush a wash of thinned latex paint over any raw, untreated wood, then go back over it with a damp paintbrush and a cotton cloth. For a finishing touch, red wax, applied just to the edges of the peg rail, adds depth.

PREPARATION

First remove the pegs: they will be painted separately and replaced when dry. Sand the rack and pegs to a smooth finish and wipe with a tack cloth to remove loose particles. Apply a coat of clear, quick-drying wood preservative and allow to dry thoroughly.

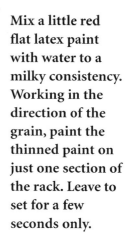

Mix a little red flat latex paint with water to a milky consistency. Working in the direction of the grain, paint the thinned paint on just one section of the rack. Leave to set for a few seconds only.

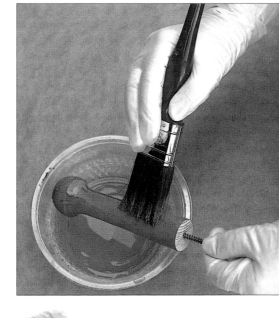

Mix a small amount of yellow flat latex paint with water to a milky consistency. Carefully paint the diluted yellow paint over the red pegs, turning them orange.

Pick up a small amount of red wax on some cotton cloth and apply it just to the edges of the rack.

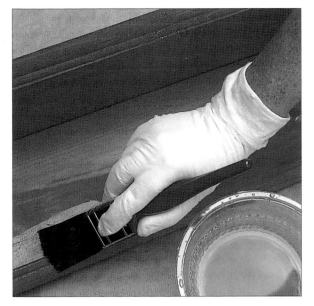

 Work a clean, slightly damp paintbrush over the still-wet paint to dilute the color further.

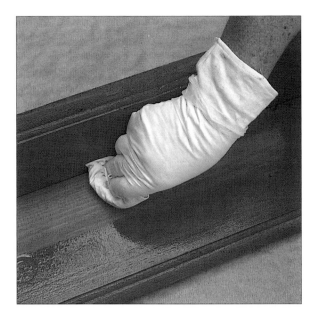

Wipe a pad of dry, clean cotton cloth over the painted surface to remove any excess wash. Complete the rest of the rack, including the pegs, following Steps 1–3, and leave everything to dry.

Buff the wax to a soft sheen with some fine-grade steel wool. Allow to dry overnight before protecting with two coats of extra pale dead flat oil-based varnish, letting the first coat dry overnight before applying the second.

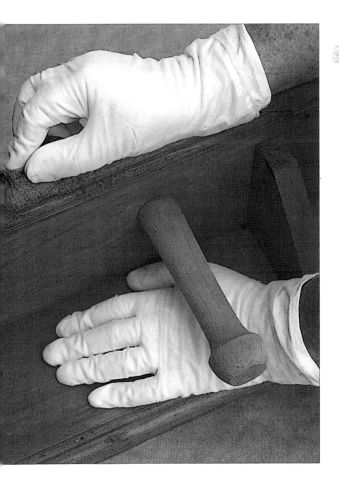

ALTERNATIVE
You could use two different-colored washes all over the woodwork, in the same way as the pegs have been treated. Some possible combinations to experiment with are blue and green, red and yellow or mauve and blue.

FREEHAND PAINTING AND STAMPING GARDEN TRUGS

The humble trug is useful for holding all sorts of garden paraphernalia; pruning shears and seed packets, twine and twigs, bulbs and weeds often rest there, but the trug itself is usuallly overlooked. By adding some simple decoration you can transform this practical object into a stylish piece of garden equipment.

Materials and equipment
Garden trug
2 angled fitch brushes
Pale blue-green flat latex paint
Blue-green flat latex paint

FREEHAND PAINTING
Lead pencil
Eraser
Assorted artists' acrylic colors
Fine artists' paintbrush

STAMPING
Deep blue-green stamping paint
Small foam roller
Floral stamp

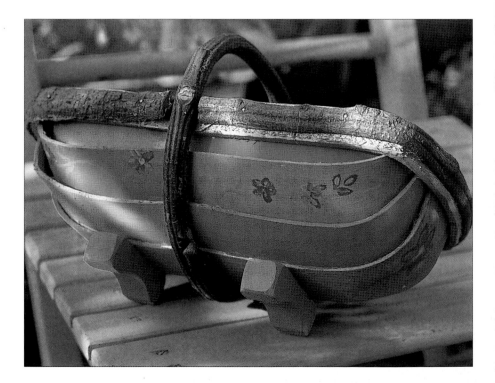

Simple floral motifs look good on subtle or brightly colored backgrounds. Experiment with possible color combinations on paper before you finally commit to your trug.

PAINTED FINISH

The decoration on the body of the trug is kept simple by using plain matte paints in just two, closely toned colors. A touch of individuality is brought in, however, with the addition of some hand-painted flowers and leaves, or some delicate stamped flower motifs.

PREPARATION

You can paint directly onto the trug but must first make sure it is clean and completely grease free.

FREEHAND PAINTING

1 On a flat surface, turn the trug over so the base is facing upward. Use an angled fitch brush to paint pale blue-green flat latex paint on alternate slats.

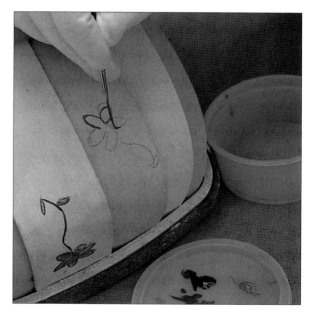

4 Pour small amounts of artists' acrylic colors onto a flat container and use a fine artists' brush to paint in the motifs. Use a deep shade for the edges of the flowers, lightening it with white as you near the center.

Delicate flowers, painted freehand, can be as elaborate or as simple as you like. Even the most naive design adds charm to the trug.

Fill in the unpainted slats and the trug stand with a deeper blue-green flat latex paint. Leave to dry.

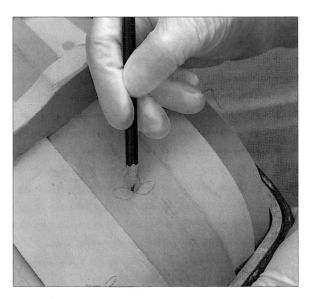

Using a sharp lead pencil, draw some simple flower, stem and leaf motifs on the slats of the trug, spacing the designs randomly. Erase any mistakes.

STAMPING

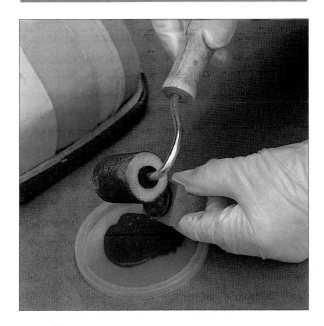

Pour a little stamping paint into a flat container. Coat a small foam roller with paint and roll it over the stamp, evenly covering it.

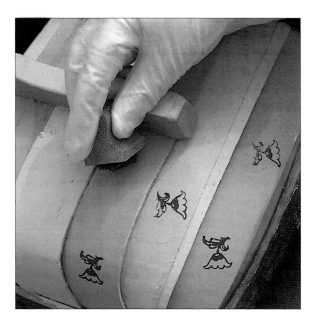

Press the stamp firmly against the trug, holding it in place for a few seconds. Recoat the stamp with paint before each imprint.

BAGGING AND SPARKLE VARNISHING TERRA-COTTA POTS

If you let your imagination stray a little, you can see that terra-cotta pots make excellent outdoor candleholders, protecting the flame from the slightest breeze.

Materials and equipment

Terra-cotta pot
2 general-purpose paintbrushes
Plaster pink smooth water-based masonry paint
Angled fitch brush
Copper metallic water-based paint
Burnt sienna artists' acrylic color
Acrylic glaze
Damp cloth
Plastic wrap
Sparkle dust
Satin acrylic varnish
2 varnish brushes
Satin polyurethane varnish
Mineral spirits for cleaning varnish brush

There are an endless number of color combinations you could use on your pots. Pictured on the left is the pot decorated in the following steps.
Pictured opposite are some other examples to light your way.
Clockwise from left:
Mid-blue base coat, silver rim, glaze mixed with cobalt blue and alizarin crimson artists' acrylic colors, sparkle dust in varnish;
Dusty pink masonry paint;
Mid-orange base coat, glaze mixed with deep red-orange masonry paint, sparkle dust in varnish;
Olive green base coat, glaze mixed with gold-yellow masonry paint, sparkle dust in varnish;
Cobalt blue base coat, yellow-gold rim, glaze mixed with sapphire blue liquid gem acrylic, sparkle dust in varnish.

CRAZED AND SPARKLE FINISH

A wonderfully crunchy, crazed texture is achieved by manipulating a tinted acrylic glaze with scrunched-up plastic wrap. The *pièce de résistance*, however, has to be the final layer of sparkle varnish, which shimmers and glitters with the changing light. The combination of colors you choose can be bright or subdued, and the addition of a painted metallic band around the rim of the pot adds a touch of drama.

PREPARATION

Specially created paint for outdoor use can be applied directly onto terra-cotta, which means that preparation of your pot is minimal. Make sure the pot is clean and dry, before applying the base coat.

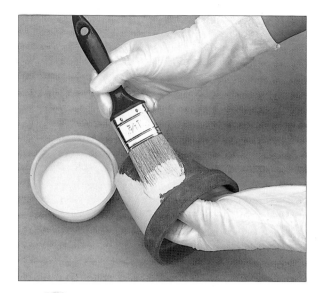

1 Use a paintbrush to apply a coat of plaster pink smooth water-based masonry paint to the outside of the pot. If necessary, apply a second coat when the first is dry.

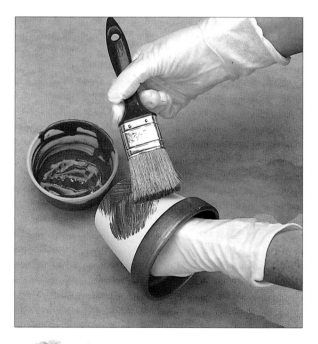

4 Use a paintbrush to roughly paint on the glaze. Clean off any glaze from the dry copper rim with a damp cloth.

ALTERNATIVES

As an alternative to sparkle dust, you could mix some liquid gem acrylic into acrylic glaze and apply it in the same way.

•

You can make a glaze in any color you want by mixing it with a small quantity of any water-based paint.

•

Adapt a large terra-cotta pot for floating candles by standing a glass container filled with water inside the pot.

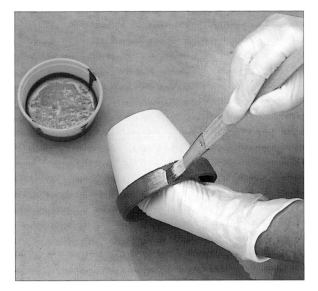

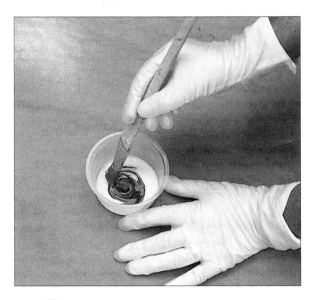

 Use an angled fitch brush to paint copper metallic water-based paint around the rim of the pot and about 2in (5cm) down inside it. Leave to dry thoroughly.

 Mix a small amount of strongly colored glaze: add just a squeeze of burnt sienna artists' acrylic color to about 2tsps (10ml) of acrylic glaze and mix together well with a brush.

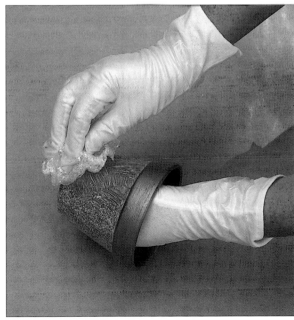

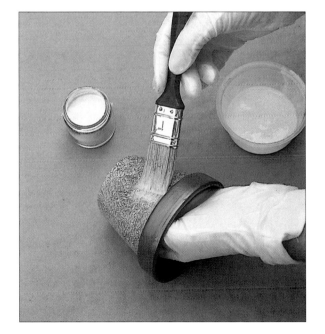

 Holding the pot from the inside, take a pad of scrunched-up plastic wrap and gently pat and roll it over the wet glaze, creating a crazed effect over the whole surface. Allow to dry thoroughly overnight.

 To make a glittery top coat, mix a little sparkle dust into some satin acrylic varnish and use a varnish brush to paint it over the crazed surface, avoiding the metallic rim. The varnish will dry clear. For added protection, seal the pot with a coat of satin polyurethane varnish.

INDEX

SUPPLIERS

Art Supply Stores
(specialty paints and mediums, artists' paintbrushes and tools, leafing supplies, patina solutions)

Craft Supply Stores
(artist's paintbrushes and tools, artists' oil paints and mediums, acrylic paints and mediums, leafing supplies, patina solutions, statuary, garden accessories)

Garden Centers
(terra-cotta pots, clay and plaster statuary, plastic pots and statuary, garden furniture and accessories)

Home Improvement Centers
(paints, primers, sealers, paintbrushes, general painting supplies, garden furniture and accessories)

The Art Store
(nationwide locations)
www.artstores.com
(Artist's oils and acrylic paints and tools; patina solutions)

DecoArt
P.O. Box 386
Stanford, Kentucky 40484
(606) 365-3193
www.decoart.com
(manufacturer and distributor of acrylic paints and specialty finishes; available in art and craft supply stores nationwide)

Johnson Paint Company
355 Newbury Street
Boston, MA. 02115
(617) 536-4244
www.johnsonpaint.com
(comprehensive collection of fine quality painting tools and supplies for faux finishing, including specialty paints, glazes, varnishes, crackle medium, craquelure, and gilding supplies)

Liquitex
Binney and Smith Inc.
1100 Church Lane
P.O. Box 431
Easton, Pennsylvania 18044
(610) 253-6271
www.liquitex.com
(manufacturer and distributor of artists' acrylic paints, varnishes, mediums, and wood stains)

Michaels Stores
(nationwide locations)
www.michaels.com
(artist's oils and acrylic paints and tools, gilding supplies, patina solutions, statuary, garden accessories)

Modern Options Patina Solutions
www.modernoptions.com
(manufacturer and distributor of high quality metallic surfaces and patinas; available in art and craft supply stores nationwide)

Pearl Paint
308 Canal Street
New York
New York 10013
1-800-221-6845
(nationwide locations)
www.pearlpaint.com
(artist's oils and acrylic paints and tools, gilding supplies, patina solutions)

Spectra Paint
7615 Balboa Blvd.
Van Nuys
CA 91406
(818) 786-5610
www.spectrapaint.com
(comprehensive collection of fine quality painting tools and supplies for faux finishing, including specialty paints, glazes, varnishes, and patina solutions)

Winsor & Newton
P. O. Box 1396
Piscataway
New Jersey 08855
www.winsornewton.com
(specialty paints and mediums, artists' paintbrushes and tools)

ACKNOWLEDGEMENTS

So many people have helped to produce this book. My thanks to Gloria Nicol for her fabulous photographs, and to Deborah Schneebeli-Morell and my great neighbour and friend Dinah Thompson for allowing us to use their gardens for some of the pictures.

Thanks to the many companies and individuals who responded so generously to my requests for project items and materials used in the book, including: Akzo Nobel Ltd; Brannam Pottery; Bridge Nursey; Casa Paints; Charlotte Fraser at Colart; Corixa Communications; The Cotswold Company; Craig and Rose plc; Cuprinol; The English Stamp Company; Geedon Ltd; Michael Venus at A.S. Handover; Jocasta Innes Paint Magic; Lotus Water Garden Products; Georgina McLaren PR; Parlane; Plasti-Kote Ltd; Plysu Brands Ltd; Polyvine Ltd; Herman Reich at Liquitex International; Scotts of Stowe; David Manuel and Annie Sloan; The Stencil Library; Stewart Ltd; Stransky Thompson; Ward Bekker Ltd; W. Zinnser. If I have neglected to mention anyone, I apologize.

I owe a debt of gratitude to my husband, Andrew, for his constant support, encouragement and practical help and to my daughter, Lucy, for her artistic advice and assistance.

Last but not least, my thanks to Melinda Coss, for persuading me to write this book and for her continued encouragement.